Broken

Loki

Loki Wizart
poems & epigram

LOKI WIZART LLC

COPYRIGHT

THE TITLE

Broken Loki refers to the many sad and heart broken stories shared to me, including the love journeys I've traveled to arrive here.

I've always had a good Listening ear and a soft heart for women. Their glory, their pain, their complicities, all of which make them extraordinary.

The poems and verses of this book was written to express my journal of love and hate, as well as the pleasure and pain of those who gifted me with their personal stories. The works of this book is only an art form and can be universally understood.

Forgive me if anything stings, I have also been stung.

THE ART

The central artwork tells a captivating tale. It depicts two hearts, one pointing upward and the other downward, symbolizing the ups and downs of a relationship. The cracks that stretch from the hands represent the point of breaking, but the hands coming together in union hold everything together. The artwork masterfully illustrates the complexities and beauty of relationships, capturing the essence of the human experience.

CHAPTERS

BLACK

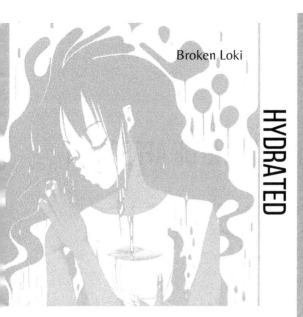

Broken Loki

HYDRATED

i cried to flood my heart
washing my feelings away-
i cried to quench
my thirst so i wouldn't
dehydrate-
staying with you is dying
accepting death over life-
and to live is to die
but with you life isn't life-

Loki Wizart

UNSPOKEN BOND OF AFFECTION

i heard,
but i didn't understand-
looking into your eyes
not knowing
what to see-
holding your hands,
unlearned of
what love could be-
time awarded me wisdom
that removed ignorance's veil-
i now know the way
but the relationship
has sailed-

Loki Wizart

tantrums replaced words
you felt but couldn't say-
not every word can equate
to the moods you embrace-
complicated when elevated,
that mouth of yours-
could sink a relationship
with those verbal swords-

VERBAL SWORDS

Loki Wizart

Broken Loki

i was the match,
the balance to your chaos-
confined between dimensions
a prison to my eclectic mind-
there were signs
i only fantasized to cherish us-
with ideas trapped in my temples,
hallucinating love-

LOVES LESSONS AND NEW BEGINNINGS

i can only wish you well
to be loved as love should allow-
and i'll use this knowledge
to love another
the way you taught me how-

waited forever to find you,
only to lose you,
too soon-
chasing my shadow
into an abandoned heart,
clinging to an old fling-
assuming i had you
by not having you,
thinking the charm would
charm-
my resentment,
i knew you were perfect,
i knew you were before
i was ready for you,
it wasn't worth it-

ECHOES OF LOVE FADING AWAY

THE WALL OF COMFORT

dysfunction
was before us
revealing a wall,
impossible to ascend-
fearful to search beyond,
willing to subdue to pursue
a life to feel a part of life-
and that is why i chose you
and failed-

Loki Wizart

i fell in love and bruised my knee-
no one, not a soul, heard me weep-
brighter nights, darker days
insomnia embraces me-
daring me to rest,
curses me with unease-

STUMBLING

9

Loki Wizart

that led to a song,
which turned into a
kiss-
moments as this,
worry-free,
with memories i miss-
there was a time
my mind
and my eyes,
belonged to you-
if you called,
i'd stop my world
to see you bloom-

blossom in the
autumn,
rain in the spring-
freezing the summer,
still, a bird would
sing-
now the leaves don't
wither
and the snow is hot-
with dry rain
neglecting
a flower cracking the
pot-
what was is now an
awakened dream,
at peace with the
moment-
the gift of the present
never stolen.

SEASON

i felt it in your soul-
with every step roaming
the icy corridors of
loneliness and sorrow-
energies matched as
a two-headed coin-
i recognized the emotion
i, too, was drenched in anguish-
unselfishly i spoke to the
sadness in you, thinking
one friend would rearrange
your frowning lipgloss
of gloomy protections,
sadness is addictive
drawing one
in the same-

BROKEN MAGNET

you abandoned my heart,
faulting me for giving my love
and affection,
my motives were modest
as you used me
as a placeholder
until the beholder
emerged-
my heroism
to strengthen your esteem-
building you into
the queen
for your so-called
dream king-
he who assumes
that you are pure,
untouched, and clean.

USER ERROR

Loki Wizart

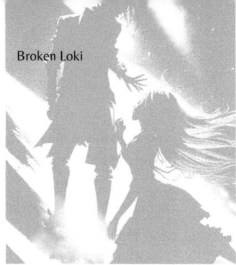

FLYING AWAY

Broken Loki

i felt your hate
the moment i embraced myself,
cutting the strings,
ignoring your songs of deception-
discovering my wings, flying away-
my touch was slipping from your grasp
the tightest you've ever held me
was when i said goodbye-
i was never expected to grow
out of the vast you planted me in,
blossoming beyond the edges,
jealous i'd be loved
the way i loved you.

Loki Mozart

Broken Loki

TEMPORARY PUPPET

because i didn't love myself
i gave you the love that i needed,
expecting to see the return-
pumped me with your stories
to stir my heart
seeking to drag me into your world,
bored of your targets
missed by cupids arrows-
i was faithful to the idea,
willing to risk it all
ignoring the flames burning my
fingers
tips every time i reached for you-
seeking gold in an empty basket
i fell into your imagination,
hoping to survive the masses
to prove my love as pure-

Loki Wizart

LOST THE SPARK

after you learned to love me,
your comfort zone expanded,
and you became the bandit
of this heart-
as time went by,
more was demanded,
but less was granted-
flickering as you lost
your spark-

i loved who you were,
not who you are-
you wanted to be loved,
i noticed your grace-
discovering your essence,
i wanted a taste-
stingy for you,
nothing hindered the pursuit-
my admiration,
where you were, so was i-
but where am you are not-
unable to be here when i need you,
quietly dying, hiding behind
my happy frown-

I LOVED

16

Broken Loki

TOGETHER ALONE

together but alone,
my heart whispers
as i envy the stare,
the glare in your pupils
as your eyes
shift lanes, drifting down
many roads-
at men who may fit
your idol-
amazing how
soft your eyes
are to strangers,
oblivious of you-
have mercy on me,
abandon me too as
your eyes do-

Loki Mozart

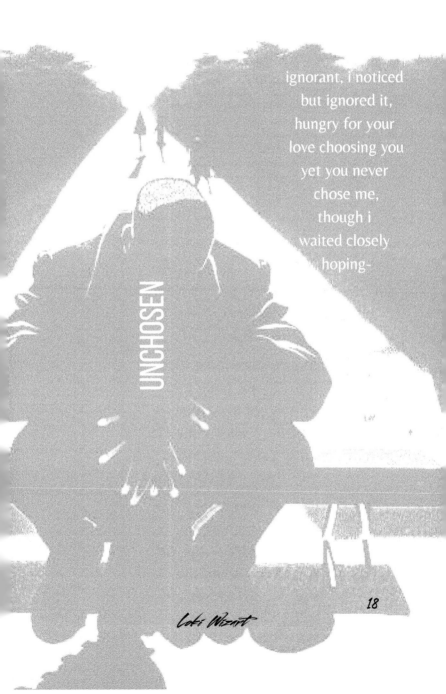

Broken Loki

ignorant, i noticed
but ignored it,
hungry for your
love choosing you
yet you never
chose me,
though i
waited closely
hoping-

UNCHOSEN

18

Loki Wizart

Broken Loki

ENDURE

trimming the edges,
the branches
of my esteem,
supposedly
i am yours truly-
so hard to trust you
but my seeds
inhibit me
the idea of freedom,
to choose me over you,
so i withstand-

Loki Wizart

19

I thirst with you,
draining myself
So The seeds
grow with infinite
waters

Loki Wizart

you lust me
not to trust me -
parting your sea
for me to swim-
closing your heart
disrobing your robe-
supposing i'd stay
rather than roam the globe-
i wanted your heart,
be it always,
so every day would be a rove-
abounding in love without sunder
under a windy night sailing
the swells-

ALWAYS >NEVER

CLARITY

am i to love your body,
or your mind-
share your notions, unbiased
sad, mad, or kind-
don't kiss me,
silencing your
voice-
don't hug me,
shunning adore
hesitant with love's choice-
to be bare is to trust, beyond
lust-
a gift unwrapped for us-
intimacy unites our souls
our language
give us clarity, to hold
the relationship in honor-
never to wander-
until you choose
to show your true love-
i will only be a follower-

Loki Wizart

She broke me,
shattering my heart
with a smile of gold
but a heart of mold

Loki Mozart

Broken Loki

FOR NOTHINGS

i breathed
my last breathe
into her-
giving the life i needed,
only for her to live on
to love another-

24

Loki Wizart

WHITE

CLIPPING WINGS

no one cares,
but he,
the so called lover,
that knows you are there-
when he weeps, when he
creeps
when he awake from his sleep-
unique-
you are, the unselfish love,
the one he doesn't see,-
but hates for you to
give your affection to
another-
afraid no one will be as patient
to his moods,
or listen to the cries,
he clips your wings
so you will never fly-

Loki Wizart

MISCOMMUNICATION

he doesn't care; he sits there
and doesn't notice me,
she thinks-
as she's
emotionally crashing,
with insecurities as
thoughts drown her mind,
she weeps-
one sound could reshape
this moment;
internally she speaks,
choosing to wait
for his reaction-
foreign to her
body language,
her face shows a blank
expression-
the stillness can't
explain her pain,
ashamed to show her
anxieties-
so he's the blame for not
noticing-
suddenly he tried
to grab her waist,
but she pulled away;
he questioned her,
are you ok,
she croaked. i'm ok.-
are you sure,
i said i'm cool,
do what you do-
now he's bothered,
troubled that she
rejected his touch-

Loki Wizart

Broken Loki

distance is a departure,
not a test-
if they wanted you,
the loneliness you'd never find
the time you'd never waste
and silence you'd never feel-
nothing is forever
even the love you think you have-
never owned, only borrowed
give it back when the time arrives-

28

Loki Wizart

Broken Loki

SHE WAITS

he waits as if forever
is much better-
however,
forever may never be-
life gives but a certain
amount
to do whatever-
so marriage must be it
now or never
or forever
hold your peace-

Loki Mozart

29

thoughts heavily roam her
mind,
as recurring dreams are
drifting,
of life beyond the barriers.-
her moods change daily,
separating the illusions
from reality
like oil, and water.-
boring chapter in her story,
ripping pages as she turns
violently.-
this can't be life; what more
is there?
she asks herself,-

as her lover sits near,
unaware of her mindset.-
she never thought to utter,
brushing his ear lobes
with her frustrations.
assuming everything's ok,
he takes the silence as a
blessing.-

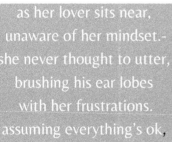

LANGUAGE BARRIER

30

Loki Wizart

Broken Loki

you crave to be seen,
but afraid to be seen
from within-
with assertions of self-worth
protecting your ego
making everyone
the blame for your mistakes,
you've become
a clone of what society
states of beauty-
ignoring that
loveliness within you,
afraid of your image
and your actions,
avoiding the mirror-

FEAR OF MIRRORS

Loki Wizart

SAYING I LOVE

Broken Loki

saying i love you,
the frequency vibrates your chest,
only when you accept it
will the journey become a test-
to love is a sacrifice,
giving what you can
to not lose it-
laying the bricks as you walk
learning moment to moment -
to step together,
dancing to the same music.

Loki Wizart

Broken Loki

silent in the presence of the loudest
he yells, you become numb-
humble, I let you yell to me
with hallucinations, confusing
me with him-
wishing without reacting,
you could display your
strength against him-
frozen are your nerves,
locked when he's near, tensed,
afraid of the unexpected-
you hate him, but emotionally,
you are trapped, reminding
lently,
financially need him-

SILENT AROUND LIONS

Loki Wizart

Broken Loki

your mind plays games
with your heart
while your heart plays games
with your soul-
running from the shadow of self,
a glimpse of light reflecting your soul,
makes you shameful-
it's ok not to be accepted
it's ok not to be perfect-
not everyone will see you
as the ideal of their eye-

SELF DEFEAT

RUSHING

over chasing your heart,
means that
you were running from me,
avoiding sincere love,
evading my company-
the selfish deception of
mine,
expecting you to mend
my loneliness -
deciding to choose you,
even though
you never chose me-
driving you away with
eagerness to
fill my emptiness,
to soothe my needs,
with fantasies
without giving you
a chance to be free-

Loki Wizart

35

he broke you,
made a joke of you,
didn't care how he
spoke to you-
the happiness you never
knew

LYING TO YOURSELF

so pain seems natural-
any attention makes you
feel
valued and approved-
even if it's the worst
affection
to consume-
unravel your soul ties
or remain tied
to the suffering-
in the shadows,
staining your pillow
with tearful mascara,
lying to yourself
of his nonsense-

36

Loki Wizart

Broken Loki

SILLY ME SAD.

maybe she wasn't in her right mind
kissing me, uttering love spells,
missing his pain-
sacrificing myself to be of service
to her wounded heart-
knowing that time heals
but revealing our deepest sorrows-
maybe i needed a friend too,
drifting in the same air
that her hair blew in-

Loki Wizart

37

Broken Loki

he hit her. she spoke,
and i listened-
my ears hugged her heart
during her moment
of feeling vulnerable-
i never expected anything
seeing her sitting alone, sadly.-
i thought she needed a friend
unconditionally; why me-
i wanted to feel her pain
rather than be alone-

SAD ATTRACTIONS

Loki Wizart

Broken Loki

FOREVER NEVER

a hug made us melt,
the word love gave us depth-
obligated to the terms,
drifting in the ship of relations-
over time we lose patience,
frowns started shaping-
saying i love you, the broken record,
contemplating turning the station-
working long days,
with short night fights,
wild intimacy replaced
with tired quickies, what a life-
it's nobody's fault for fake
expectations of the unknown
forever never, but the present is born
forever never, but life must go on-

39

Loki Wizart

Broken Loki

MASCULINITY

unwilling to let him lead,
her significant other,
she never knew that she should,
taught by a mother,
indoctrinated in independency,
limited by trauma-
a father that left the mother
to keep his dignity,
forsaking the child.-
welcoming intimacy,
tying the souls,
but rejecting matrimony
the emotional tug of wars,
with hints of lust, love and hate-
misleading because of
the lack understanding-

40

Loki Wizart

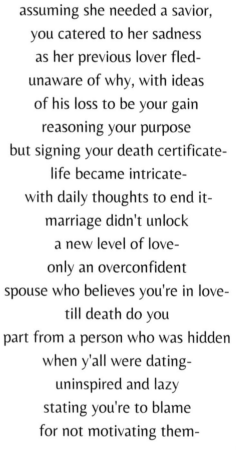

Broken Loki

assuming she needed a savior,
you catered to her sadness
as her previous lover fled-
unaware of why, with ideas
of his loss to be your gain
reasoning your purpose
but signing your death certificate-
life became intricate-
with daily thoughts to end it-
marriage didn't unlock
a new level of love-
only an overconfident
spouse who believes you're in love-
till death do you
part from a person who was hidden
when y'all were dating-
uninspired and lazy
stating you're to blame
for not motivating them-

BECAUSE OF YOU

Loki Wizart

41

Broken Loki

you see the signs
but your interest,
motivates you to win trust-
while lust lures you,
baiting you to get eaten-
mistreated
due to your efforts being
uneven-
weakened
by every action leaking-
your energy is depleting
your heart is now bleeding-
all because of your desires
misleading-
your abandonment issues
creating
the idea of loves fantasy
stimulating-
the illusions you force on
those
of your choosing-
losing in the end
for presuming it's yours,
for the taking-

PAIN BY ASSUMPTION

42

Loki Wizart

The lie of

saying

I love you,

For sport—

only to feel

Wanted in

short,

In return

Loki Mozart

WE CHEAT

we cheat
when the consistency dies-
and lie
because we care
not to see them cry-
hard to change,
rearrange our lives-
so in the shadows
we survive and thrive-
it's not accepted
nor respected-
yet no one knows how it
feels to be rejected-
sworn to be with someone
forever-
as they hold you captive
for their pleasure-
afraid of you doing better
with another-
giving you enough
for you to stay-
but less to make it
work for their love in every way-

Loki Wizart

Broken Loki

SHADES

she loves differently,
with two shades of love-
one, what you want her to be,
the other, what she thinks of.

46

Loki Wizart

CLEANSE

sadness feels good
with a frown that smiles
and warm
tears to cleanse the mind.

Loki Wizart

The best
parts of me
got broken
when she, my queen,
smiled
at Him
with the same lips
she kissed
me with

DESTINY STOLEN

Broken Loki

the moment
things become routine,
love strikes like a lightning bolt
setting ablaze to the heart and soul-
where were you when i was alone?
why me? why now?-
you want them more,
when they are not yours-
together chosen out of vulnerability
only to see it for what it truly is
yet longing for the one who
near and dear to your heart,
but far from destiny-

Loki Wizart

49

Broken Loki

EXISTING UNBOTHERED

i asked her why,
why does she look so mad-
she told me that
she wasn't,
she is simply existing-
conveying that she's
unbothered,
i got excited-
i liked that -

50

Loki Wizart

FANTASIZING EXPECTATIONS

could love be fantasized
with no details of how
to survive beyond
the years?-
is love lazy?
to cherish a person
in the name of,
even when the scale tilts-
is love consistent
or an experiment
a curious exploration,
that perishes
when the conquest
doesn't meet the
expectation-

Loki Mozart

52

Broken Loki

a touch of shadow
to hide your eyes
behind the details
revealed behind your eyelids-
the things you see but ignore
out of sight, out of mind
with no accountability-
blush on your cheeks
without blushing
melts the heart-
causing warmth to cycles
through the veins-
eyeliner and lashes reveal
but conceal the pupils hidden
in plain view,
your shy insecurity-

SHADOWS OF UNCERTAINTY

Loki Mozart

53

AN ENDLESS SEA OF YEARNING

Broken Loki

if love never meets you,
will you be content with reality?
the reality that you
may be visually in love,
but blinded by a fantasy-
slowly swimming in an ocean
with no shore gasping
for air you will never breathe-

Loki Wizart

Broken Loki

gentle inquiries from me to you,
led to unaccountable defensive retorts-
every reason you gave drove you away
from the windows of truths-
ego with no hope for internal glow-
but the need to put on a show-
for the world to see a different
you than i-

WINDOWS OF TRUTH

Loki Wizart

55

Broken Loki

RIDING BACKWARDS INTO UNCERTAINTY

riding backward,
blindly unaware of loves obstacles,
hoping someone would see
the love given, as sacrificed-
afraid, fearful that they will see
your desperation, the lack of love
you have within, self-love-

Loki Wizart

heroic ways
tickle the ego
but hide the mind from the truth-
no matter what you invest in,
nothing is truly yours to own-
the love you give,
be prepared to lose it
to the atmosphere-

HEROES OF EGOISM

Loki Wizart

57

Broken Loki

tv fantasy has fooled you both-
she expected you to slay her dragons.
and you wanted her to love you
when she awoke-
she wanted you
to provide at her lowest point.
then begged her to stay
when you were broke-
before knowing
each other's favorite colors,
intimate ties were magical-
but after watching
the same show over time,
the channel changed-
charming became boring,
and the villain became alluring,
the adventure you've
longed to endure-

Broken Loki

does she love you,
how do you know?
because of her words,
or her reactions to your gifts?
is love eternal or a stolen moment?-
an escape from the truth
we see in a mirror hidden
behind another's attention?-
validation?

Loki Wizart

Broken Loki

when love yells,
it sounds like hate,
as a door slams
but remains open-
like snow on a sunny day,
a rainbow on a rainy night-
love could be better
if we hated each other, right?-
we miss what neglects us
and want what
we can't have-
if you say that you hate me
with a smile, i only see the smile-
if you say you love me
with a frown, i receive it-
even if you never
meant it
to stick-

Loki Wizart

Broken Loki

love takes months with conditions
but dies in seconds without
understanding, unfulfilled emotions-
placing expectations
and conditions to be met until
the efforts are reversed-
such a gamble. we will
never know how much
a person loves us.
hopeful but dumb-

EMPTY HOPE

Loki Mozart

61

Loki

fear of abandonment
you cling to grasp
and held to hold-
to anyone, who or why,
only to keep whichever
whomever you know-
mother was busy as father
abandoned home,
dating became
seeking for father-
dating turned into
loving longing for
mother's touch,
all that you've known-
banishing reality,
forcing ideas to fit
the shape of your limited
thoughts-

ABANDONMENT ISSUES

DISCOVERING STRENGTH WITHOUT SMILES OR TEARS

if the mother never smiles
and father never cries,
where did we learn
to love and how-
if love is more than
what meets the eye-
do themes deceive us
drowning our minds?-
to be upset is to care
to smile misleads-
i've had more backstabbers
smile as the sad ones
comforted me-
if love is love, how do
we know-

Loki Wizart

Broken Loki

LOVER'S HOPEFUL NOTHINGS

love is most bewitching
during the pursuit -
boredom bathes us
moments after-
hopeful nothings,
humble disasters-
good for nothing,
loving to be loved,
but loved to be hated-
neglected then baited,
played as a yoyo
until the string broke-

66

Loki Mozart

Sometimes
we put
everything
into something
that later becomes
nothing but
something

Loki Wizart

Broken Loki

mountains
of letters
misunderstood
with disregard-
guarded by pride
the broken
heart, you hid
to hide-
cracked by,
he whom you loved
by sight,
ignorant
to where his
faith lay-

MUTED PAINS

66

Broken Loki

no one is prepared
for the expectations
of another,
making attempts
to become
someone else,
for them to like you-

THE IMPOSIBLE TASK OF BEING SOMEONE ELSE'S

Loki Wizart

A HEART WISH

we want love
overlooking everything
one has to bestow -
kissing everyone
seeking that
magical kiss-
turning a frog into a
prince-

68

Loki Mozart

Broken Loki

unless we know
our destination,
the beginning ends
abruptly-
undiscovered
with no purpose,
time will slap us
with reality

ROAD TO NOWHERE

Loki Mozart

69

efforts
unleashed,
sings love
into her heart daily-
calmness and peace-
inspires
the willingness
to sacrifice his
all for her-

INSPIRATIONAL WILLINGNESS TO SACRIFICE ALL

70

Broken Loki

RUNNING AFTER A MIRAGE

stop chasing
what is evading-
supposing
the yearn for-
naive, universe
in the signs
of undesired
expressions-
riled at anyone
but the one
who fails
to notice
without emotions.

71

Loki Mozart

Broken Loki

agonizing,
melting your soul-
eroding the hours
longing for him,
burning in the cold
scorned by his
detachment,
with stoic words
and unfeeling actions-

FROZEN EMOTIONS

72

Loki Wizart

affectionate
words bring
comfort to
hopeful ears,
but lazy ways
are like
apathetic actions-
betraying the ears,
while neglecting
a gnawing, starving
heart that
seeks love-

EMPTY PROMISES

73

Broken Loki

LOVES MAZE

shall one suffer
to keep another happy
while they deny
self-happiness?
suppressing feelings
above their own,
yet locked in a
maze of mysteries,
unknown-
questioning
if love is truly a lie,
blocking the doubt
of trueness
in front of
your eyes-

Loki Wizart

74

Broken Loki

SHATTERED DREAMS & EMOTIONAL RIFTS

my thoughts scatter
like glass shatters,
as the dryness of your
text enters. i gaze-
the mood shift
with the riffs
of your voice tone
as it rips me
emotionally-
yet and still
i'm supposed to
love you, beyond
the bitterness-

Loki Wizart

loneliness aches,
and pulsates
the heart-
mostly
when you are
spoken for
but spoken-less-
inside but outside-
cast yet outcast-
by the one
who is supposed
to make us whole. -

SURROUNDED YET ALONE

76

Loki Mozart

I never knew what
loneliness felt like
until I whispered I
love you to her, my
love, listening to the
Echos as the steamy
breathe floated from
my lips—

Loki Wizart

THE GLOOM OF
THE DAY,
SHOULDN'T STOP
YOUR JOURNEY,
THE WILLINGNESS
OF WALKING
AWAY.

Loki Wizart

Broken Loki

our tales of pity,
clever, witty and gritty-
but easy,
on the ears-
an emotional symphony-
when you're down,
you send for me-
as you demolish
me without reasoning-
the clown
with a frown,
inevitably-
too kind to
and blind to
to flee this capsule freely.

Loki Wizart

THE WITTY SYMPHONY OF GRITTY PITY

SILENT FEAR OF LONELINESS

a dark field of chagrin,
with winds of anxiety swirling
in
and grazing your mind,
accusing those too close,
compassionate and kind.
assuming the world is
against you far and wide,
afraid that your insecure
heart will open and unwind.
soon you'll be stunned
and surprised,
with nowhere to run,
impossible to hide.
no one in sight
for your misleading hollow
cries,
no one to blame,
so you will and must change,
bringing an end to your
games,
the shame, the pain,
unchained.

81

Loki Mozart

relationship beginnings
are fulfilling,
with smiles and laughter
favorably winning.
never a moment,
like sunny nights and
moony mornings,
everything's perfect
not counting the blessings.

until comfort sets in
and the unmasking begins
what was once cute
now thought of as annoying
i love you became a routine
suddenly the saying is boring
is it that we fool ourselves
wanting to be wanted
fitting what stories tale of love?
frustrated when the pages
are differently illustrated
of the efforts needed for love?

FOOLING OURSELVES IN LOVE

Loki Mozart

Broken Loki

empty mornings in my vacant bed,
keeping the curtains closed
to shut out the blinding light,
and loud thoughts in my head.
give unto me the feeling
of stillness in the night,
unbothered dwelling in my room,
my cocoon.
uninterested in food or to move,
i just want to lay here,
and count the years.
i played myself
to be played with, loving me
with your ideas and fears,
of being alone
for the rest of your years.
i just wanted to love someone
as you wanted someone to love you
choosing me out of urgency
just to say you have a boo.
but i remain stuck in this empty bed,
room
my cocoon of comfort my only frien
as i lay here and count the years
and dwell in this stillness until the en

Loki Mozart

UNANSWERED LONGING OF LOVE

Broken Loki

THE NOW OF REFUGE

it will become lucid
in the instant
they escape,
see,
it's hard to explore
beyond the yellow tape,
buried in the mud
of your abandonment ruts,
as thwarting obstructs
becoming ruinous to your strut.

Loki Wizart

let it pour like honey
from your mouth,
before the candle
flickers and douse,
sing out your love
with a passionate
refrain,
declaring your love
to them
with sincere serenade,
exhale the verse
before the flame
burns out and fades,
with the last breath,
seize this moment
before it's too late.

SING BEFORE YOU GO

Loki Mozart

85

he is one of those,
the wannabes,
the ones who lives
as if he knows,
everything but
can't do anything
without her show,
shining in her glow,
her financial flow,
even though
he swears by his brow,
he's the man of the hour,
knowing if he loses her,
his flamboyant life
will be devoured-

LIVING HIS BEST LIFE

86

Loki Mozart

Broken Loki

lies hoarder,
hiding behind apprehension-
overreaction's outcry
with every shameful
remembrance-
blissful ignorance,
creates a happy idiot-
with casual sex and regular meals,
derailing your ambitions-

THE ILLUSION OF HAPPINESS

Loki Wizart

Broken Loki

open flames cracking
like a broken heart
forsaken,
love is an ocean
filled to the rim,
abundant for those
willing to swim
for the taken,
devastated are many,
whose love was mistaken,
because others who were faking,
the challenges we face when
we search for love in others places,
when love true love,
is within us in all spaces

THE SEARCH FOR TRUE LOVE

Loki Wizart

is it so hard to
admit to
the pain you spew-
through the tips
of your lips-
stirring emotional brews-
scaring hearts with
invisible bruises,
that scar deeper
than the reaper,
to anyone of your choosing-
account for the broken-
hearted,
the esteems you've
slaughtered-
most will never be the same,
living with a heart harden
from all the pain-

CRUEL WORDS

Loki Wizart

CAUGHT IN THE CLOAKING OF MISFORTUNE

heavy drapes close
to go unseen,
when we sense
despair and helplessness,
uninspired and
unfocused-
fooled by the hocus
pocus of deceitful culprits-
targeted by the haughty,
stalking us-
like a merciless eagle
to a frail rabbit,

seeking to conquer us-
out of habit,
for they too mock us-
helplessly scurrying
in a box of their
own shadows,
vulnerable as us,
hiding behind
the hint of ominous.
we seek solace in
the dark abyss
daring to one day
spread our wings to fly
to the beacon of hope.

Loki Wizart

UNCLOUDED SIGHT

the beauty
of her face
doesn't mean
the moral
of her way
is loyal

nothing
can replace
the orals
spoken torpedos
that burrow
holes
in one's soul

of another
whose love
was bold
and out of
control

probe
her globe
to discover
her mode
of motive
to be sold

once
you know
and it unfolds

find the
power inside
to let go
and not hide

those blinded
eyes
from a lie
that twines
the mind

restricting
the light
and igniting
the flame
of truth
from your sight

like the cloudy
skies hugging
moon light
to hide
the truth
her games right
in front of you
with a swap
of your sight

91

Loki Wizart

he stole
that part of you
from your clutch,
vulnerable to his
allure,
there's nothing
wrong with
trialling
with lust, but
when
your heart
ensnares
others cease
to care much,

rebuild
restore
your heart
those things in
your chest
which he ripped
apart,
you got this
lioness
roar to soar
causing savages
to vanish ,
protect yourself at
all cost
for turmoil and
anguish-

forgive yourself
and spread your
wings
become more
than an image,
discover the
power
that draws the
force of life
to you
unlock the
courage that lies
within
and rise up from
the ashes
again-

PHOENIX RISING

92

Loki Wizart

When a crow
no longer soar
only then
will a broken heart

weep

Loki Wizart

Broken Loki

LIES OF TODAY, TOMORROWS TRUTH

Loki Wizard

if loves,
enrapture bask today,
no one, in love,
would ensure
a heartbreak
of sorrow,
a love on display
shown on replay
while the heart
is in dismay
drained
before and after
this day
14th of february
the lies of today
reveals the truths
of tomorrow
after we
awake

94

Broken Loki

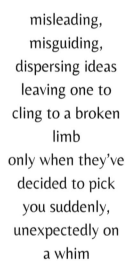

goodbyes
have two sides,
to see you later
or next lifetime

to see you soon
or venture through
the spheres of time
and the grandeur
of my mind

A LETTING GO OF GOODBYES

if anyone wants you
chance
would be a stranger's
danger
to hope

filling your head
like a balloon
with admiration,
like a star-studded
soap

misleading,
misguiding,
dispersing ideas
leaving one to
cling to a broken
limb
only when they've
decided to pick
you suddenly,
unexpectedly on
a whim

Loki Wizart

UNMASKED TIME

people choose their love;
or lust the idea of,
who's pretty on the eyes:
with luxury buys,
stability and who knows why,
then hate them for their motive.
actions and treatment
living in a disguise
unmasked only in time.

96

Loki Wizart

SLY MOUNTAIN

mountains never sway
the way you flee
from love and conflict,
unloyal they bear together
through the rain
every moment,
a battle of pain.

97

Loki Wizart

i thank you wholeheartedly

ABOUT THE AUTHOR

Loki Wizart is a talented author and poet known for his unique perspective on love and heartbreak. His writing explores the complexity of human emotions, delving into the sadness of love and the unexpected happiness that can be found in heartbreak. He draws inspiration from his introverted and empathetic nature, using the void, darkness, and unknown as a source of creativity and energy. Writing anonymously allows him to freely express his thoughts and emotions without the constraints of societal expectations. His work is both powerful and thought-provoking, resonating with readers who have experienced the ups and downs of love and heartbreak.

LET'S CONNECT

WWW.LokiWizartPoetry.com

IG: LokiWizartPoetry

TikTok: LokiWizartPoetry

Email: Tilo@LokiWizartPoetry.com

The inverted
smile, she hides,
And the gorgeous
gloom Of her
Heart is my
Addiction.
I Challenge
Myself
relentlessly
to Invert the frown,
Leading me to
Endless
Quests
Of Her soul
To love
-sad girl